27.07

3/06

MAMMOTHS AND MASTODONS

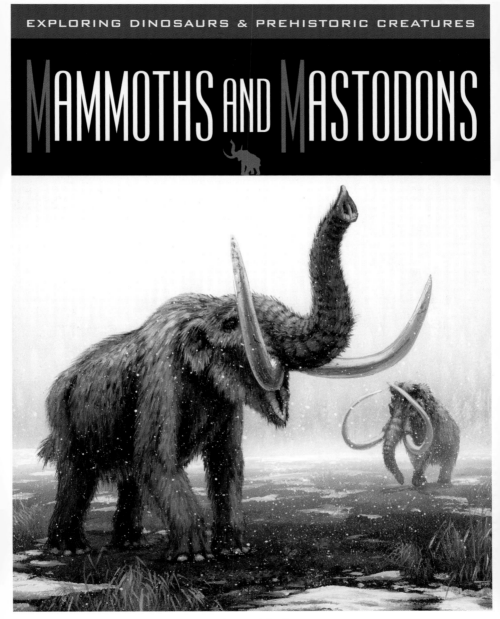

By Susan H. Gray

The Child's World®

Published in the United States of America by The Child's World®
PO Box 326, Chanhassen, MN 55317-0326
800-599-READ
www.childsworld.com

*Content Adviser:
Brian Huber, PhD,
Curator, Department
of Paleobiology,
Smithsonian
National Museum
of Natural History,
Washington DC*

Photo Credits: Nancy Palmieri/AP/Wide World Photos: 13; Tim Thompson/Corbis: 15; Soqui Ted/Corbis Sygma: 17; Reuters/Corbis: 19; Eric and David Hosking/Corbis: 23; Bettmann/Corbis: 25, 27; Mike Fredericks: 5, 24; Douglas Henderson: 22; Roger Viollet/Getty Images: 12; Indiana State Museum and Historic Sites, artist Karen Carr: 4; Michael Long/The Natural History Museum, London: 6, 7; The Natural History Museum, London: 11; North Wind Picture Archives: 14; Albert Copley/Visuals Unlimited: 9, 10; David Wrobel/Visuals Unlimited: 16, Glenn Oliver/Visuals Unlimited: 21.

The Child's World®: Mary Berendes, Publishing Director

Editorial Directions, Inc.: E. Russell Primm, Editorial Director; Pam Rosenberg, Line Editor; Katie Marsico, Associate Editor; Matthew Messbarger, Editorial Assistant; Susan Hindman, Copy Editor; Melissa McDaniel, Proofreader; Tim Griffin/IndexServ, Indexer; Olivia Nellums, Fact Checker; Dawn Friedman, Photo Researcher; Linda S. Koutris, Photo Selector

Original cover art by Todd Marshall

The Design Lab: Kathleen Petelinsek, Design; Kari Thornborough, Page Production

Library of Congress Cataloging-in-Publication Data
Gray, Susan Heinrichs.
  Mammoths and mastodons / by Susan H. Gray.
      p. cm. — (Exploring dinosaurs & prehistoric creatures)
  Includes index.
  ISBN 1-59296-409-5 (lib. bd. : alk. paper) 1. Mammoths—Juvenile literature.
2. Mastodon—Juvenile literature. I. Title.
  QE882.P8G73 2005
  569'.67—dc22
                                                    2004018075

TABLE OF CONTENTS

CHAPTER ONE

HAVING A COLD DRINK

The young mastodon (MASS-tuh-don) looked across the ice.

He had come here for a drink, but the pond was frozen exc

for a spot in the middle. He was really thirsty, and that spot certain

looked good. He carefully stepped out onto the ice.

Mastodons were elephant-like creatures that often lived near rivers and ponds.

It was slippery, but solid, and

he took another step. The ice

creaked a little, but it held.

He took a few more steps

when suddenly the ice

began to give way. Cracks

zigzagged across the whole

pond, and the ice under

A mastodon that broke through the ice and fell into water would have had to struggle mightily to get back onto dry land.

the mastodon collapsed. All of a sudden, the beast was up to his ears

in freezing cold water.

He struggled to turn around and then headed back toward the

bank. All of the ice was broken up into chunks now. Although his

body was covered in thick fur, he felt the bitterly cold sting of the

water. It made his muscles stiff, and he found it hard to move.

*A young mastodon grazes with adults members of its herd. Staying with the herd helped protect the young from becoming food for **predators** such as saber-toothed (SAY-bur-tootht) cats.*

The mastodon fought to make it to shore. He finally reached the

edge of the pond and stepped up onto the bank. The ground was icy

and slick, and the mastodon slid back into the pond. He tried again

and failed. Finally, he stomped onto the bank with all his might and

lunged forward with one last burst of energy. He made it. He was on solid ground. Panting heavily, he turned again toward the water.

In a minute, he would start to drink.

A herd of mammoths (MAM-uths) had watched the whole

scene from a hilltop nearby. They, too, had been on their way to

the pond, but they stopped when they heard the ice crack. Now

that the excitement was over, they moved forward again. Soon

they'd be sharing the watering hole with the exhausted mastodon.

*Mammoths lived during the last Ice Age. Some lived in regions where
the landscape was almost always covered by snow and ice.*

CHAPTER TWO

WHAT WERE MASTODONS?

Mastodons were elephant-like **mammals** that lived from about 35 million to 10,000 years ago. They were not quite as tall as modern-day elephants. At the shoulder, they measured between 7 and 10 feet (2 and 3 meters) high. As adults, they weighed between 4 and 6 tons.

The creatures had long tusks that curved slightly upward. The tusks were actually oversized teeth in the upper jaw. Some males grew an extra pair of short tusks from their lower jaw. The rest of the mastodon's teeth were built for grinding tough plant material. Each tooth had two rows of little cone-shaped bumps. Such teeth were perfect for crushing twigs, bark, and leaves.

Mastodons were stockier and more heavyset than elephants of today. They had hairy trunks, long hairy tails, and shaggy, reddish-brown fur. Their skulls were low and flat, and they had small ears.

A mastodon skeleton clearly shows the animal's tusks and teeth as well as the shape of its skull.

CHAPTER THREE

WHAT WERE MAMMOTHS?

Mammoths were also huge, elephant-like animals. They

lived from about 2 million to 10,000 years ago.

Different kinds of mammoths were different sizes. Among the

smallest was the pygmy (PIG-mee) mammoth. It was only about

Not all elephant-like animals were huge. Elephas falconeri (EL-uh-fuss fowl-KAHN-er-eye) was only about 3 feet (1 m) high at its shoulder. Fossils remains of this animal have been found on the Mediterranean islands of Sicily and Malta.

6 feet (1.8 m) tall at the shoulder and weighed nearly a ton. Among the largest was the imperial mammoth, which stood about 14 feet (4.3 m) at the shoulder and may have weighed 8 tons.

The ridges on this mammoth tooth helped the animal grind its food into small pieces.

A mammoth had a long trunk that was quite flexible. It used its trunk to grab small shrubs or bunches of grass and place them in its mouth. The tip of the trunk was sensitive and could probably pull up a single flower or a few blades of grass at a time. Mammoth teeth were the size of shoe boxes. On the surface, they had many ridges that helped them grind food to bits. Modern-day elephants have teeth with similar ridges.

The trunk dangled between two enormous tusks. The tusks grew throughout the animal's life and curved upward. In some older mammoths, they became so long that they turned inward and crossed in front of the animal.

The woolly mammoth is probably the best known of all the mammoths. It had long, coarse brown hair that covered a short undercoat of wool. Even its trunk and tail were covered in shaggy fur. Underneath the skin was a thick layer of fat that helped **insulate** the animal. The woolly mammoth also had a fat-filled hump right behind its head.

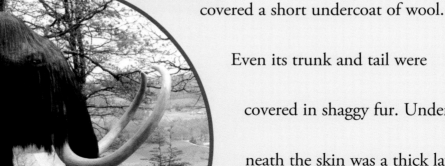

A mammoth's tusks continued to grow throughout its life. A 16-foot (5-m) long tusk was found in Texas and is on display in New York at the American Museum of Natural History.

An easy way to remember the difference between mammoths and mastodons is to think about their size. People use the word *mammoth* to mean something huge. And except for the pygmies, the mammoths were certainly huge. They were bigger than the mastodons. They had longer

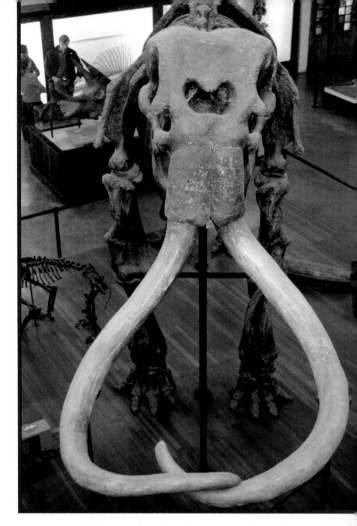

Mammoth tusks often grew so long that they began to curve inward and upward.

tusks than the mastodons, and their tusks curved more. Mammoths had taller heads, and their backs sloped more steeply toward their hips. Mammoths also had bigger ears than the mastodons. Almost every-thing about the mammoth was mammoth-sized!

CHAPTER FOUR

WHERE DID THESE
ANIMALS LIVE?

Scientists believe that the ancestors of mastodons lived in

Africa, about 35 million years ago. Over time, they spread

into Europe and then throughout Asia. About 15 million years ago,

they crossed a strip of land that connected present-day Russia and

Mastodons lived throughout the United States and Canada.

Alaska. Once they reached North America, they spread across the lands that are now Canada and the United States. They even went as far south as Mexico.

The mastodons lived wherever trees

This area at Bering Land Bridge National Preserve is part of the land bridge that once connected Asia and North America. Most of the land that bridged the two continents is now underwater.

and water were plentiful. Mastodon remains have been found near

ancient, dried-up ponds and lakes. Some have pieces of spruce,

pine, and cedar trees in their stomachs. Therefore, we know that

these animals lived near watering holes and munched on evergreens.

Like the mastodons, the first mammoths also came from Africa, but this group appeared about 4 million years ago. From Africa, they moved northward and spread throughout Europe and Asia. About 1.7 million years ago, mammoths ambled across the piece of land that connected Asia to North America at that time. Once they reached this continent, they spread into areas that had plenty of grass to eat. They

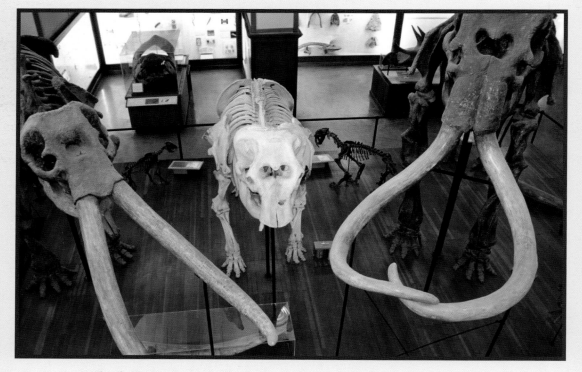

The skeletons of a mastodon (left), woolly mammoth (right), and a modern elephant (center) help demonstrate the differences between the three animals.

crossed rivers, plains, and the Rocky Mountains. They traveled all the way to present-day Mexico, Central America, Florida, and Maine.

It's likely that mammoths and mastodons saw each other from time to time. In California, mam-

Scientists dig for fossils at the La Brea Tar Pits.

moth and mastodon bones have been found in the same location. At a place called the La Brea (luh BRAY-uh) Tar Pits, scientists have discovered their remains, along with those of wolves, saber-toothed cats, and many other animals.

FROZEN IN TIME

One day in 1997, a Siberian man named Zharkov told his family he was going out for a while. The ice outside had melted a little, and Zharkov thought he'd take a look around. Little did he know that he was about to find something that would stun the scientific world.

Zharkov found a tusk sticking up from the ice. Word spread quickly about the tusk, and scientists came to look. They decided it belonged to a mammoth that had died about 23,000 years earlier. The amazing thing was that most of the creature's body was present. Its fur, skin, organs, and bones were still intact. It was as if the mammoth had been stored in a freezer for centuries.

After much planning, the scientists returned in 1999 to dig out the mammoth. They wanted to move it to a place where they could study it more easily. But the mammoth would have to stay frozen during the move.

The scientists used radar to see exactly where the mammoth rested inside the ice. Then they used jackhammers to cut trenches in the frozen soil that held the beast. Finally, they were ready to move

the icy block with the mammoth inside. But the block was out in the middle of nowhere. There were no highways or railroads nearby, so the scientists decided they needed a helicopter for the job.

The helicopter came in and hovered over the block. Workers carefully hooked the icy cargo to the aircraft. They held their breath as the helicopter lifted its 22-ton load. All went well, and later that day, the mammoth arrived at its new home—a cold, underground storage cellar in a town 200 miles (322 kilometers) away.

There, the scientists used a rack of hair dryers to slowly thaw out the animal. They found that it was a male that had been about 47 years old when it died. They looked at plants stuck to his body and decided that he died near a pond. Now named Zharkov, after the man who discovered it, the incredible mammoth will be studied for years to come.

CHAPTER FIVE

WHAT DID MAMMOTHS AND MASTODONS DO ALL DAY?

Mammoths and mastodons were enormous animals that spent much of their time eating. The mammoths, with their ridged teeth, were grazers (GRAY-zerz). They walked along, tearing clumps of grass from the ground and eating them.

Grinding down 500 pounds (227 kilograms) of food each day was not easy on mammoth teeth. In fact, mammoths often broke their teeth or wore them down. Throughout most of the animal's life, whenever an old tooth fell out, a new one came in just behind it. A mammoth grew six sets of teeth in its lifetime. As the last set wore down, the animal found it more and more difficult to eat.

The mastodons, with their bumpy teeth, were browsers (BROW-zerz). This means they fed mainly on plant materials that were higher

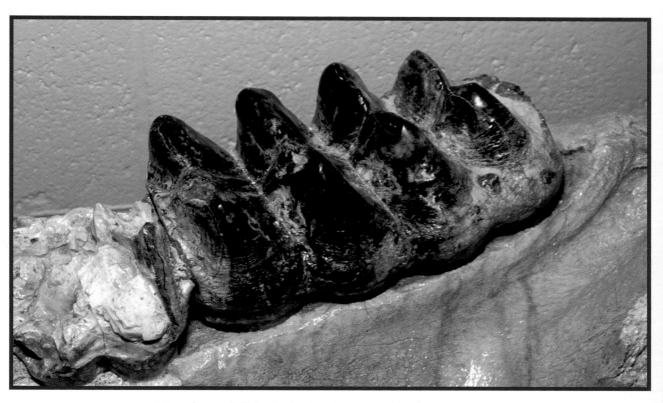

Mastodon teeth helped scientists determine that the animals were browsers—animals that feed mainly on twigs and leaves from trees.

up from the ground, such as bark, twigs, and tree leaves. Scientists

have studied mastodon droppings and found that they contain pieces

of cypress and willow trees, wild grapes, pokeweed, and wild

gourds. Cypress and willow trees grow near water, but the other

plants do not. This tells us that mastodons often fed near watering

holes, and also that they sometimes found food in dry areas.

It is likely that mammoths lived and traveled in herds much like modern-day elephants.

Mammoths probably lived and traveled in herds. Like elephants, their herds were made up of females and young only. Adult males lived on their own. Mastodons may also have lived in herds. In Texas, scientists discovered a cave that contained the skeletons of many young mastodons. The animals did not live in the cave, but they lived nearby. They were probably killed by predators, such as saber-toothed cats, and then dragged to the cave and eaten.

TASKS FOR TUSKS

Tusks were huge, heavy weights on the heads of mammoths and mastodons. They probably got in the way at times, and they often broke off. So why would these animals need such things?

Elephants today probably use their tusks in the same way that mammoths and mastodons did. Elephants use them to rip bark from trees and to dig up plants. A tusk makes a good weapon

and also a great place to rest a trunk.

Mammoths and mastodons were plant eaters. Their tusks would have come in handy for gouging the bark from trees and for uprooting small bushes and shrubs. They also would have been useful for scraping snow away from the plants below.

There are signs that the animals also used their tusks in battle. Mastodon remains show stab wounds that could have been made by tusks of other males. These males might have been battling for females, food, or space when the dreadful wounds were inflicted.

Quite often, pairs of fossilized tusks are not identical. One tusk shows more signs of wear than the other one. Just like right-handed and left-handed human beings, these ancient beasts were either right-tusked or left-tusked!

CHAPTER SIX

FINDING MAMMOTHS AND MASTODONS EVERYWHERE

You might think that scientists are always the ones who discover mammoth and mastodon remains. This is not the case, however. Many times people stumble upon fossils of these animals when they're not even looking for them.

In 1927, a street crew in Michigan found mastodon backbones, tusks, and ribs right in downtown Kalamazoo. Since then, so many mastodons have been found in Michigan that the animal was named the official state fossil.

In 1948, workers in an Alaskan gold mine came across something that

A woman displays a mastodon tusk found in Michigan in 1922.

looked like a dead elephant. It was no elephant, however. They had discovered part of the dried up and shriveled remains of a young woolly mammoth. Now named Effie, the little mammoth is kept in an Alaskan museum.

In 1989, some men in Ohio were digging a pond for a golf course. Suddenly, they ran into something hard, but it didn't seem to be a rock. It turned out that they had hit the skeleton of a mastodon, and it was one of the biggest and best skeletons ever found.

Two years later, a backhoe operator in Nova Scotia, Canada, got quite a surprise. As he lifted a load of dirt from the ground, he noticed something long and white poking out of the bucket. A closer look showed that the man had found a mastodon tusk.

In 2004, a man and his wife were walking their dog along the beach in Washington State. They saw something shiny in the sand and

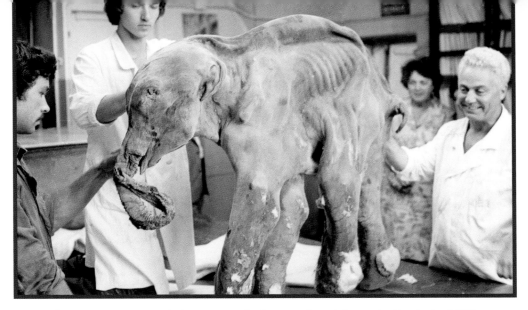

Scientists examine a baby mammoth that was found frozen in Russia in 1977.

went to see what it was. They had discovered a mammoth tusk that was 8 feet (2.4 m) long. The mammoth had probably walked along the same shore 12,000 years earlier.

Every year, people find more remains of the mammoths and mastodons that died out so long ago. We don't know what caused these great beasts to disappear. Perhaps they could not adapt to changes in the climate. Maybe diseases, shrinking food supplies, or hunters caused them to vanish. We may never know why they died, but each discovery helps us understand how they lived.

Glossary

ancient (AYN-shunt) Something that is ancient is very old; from thousands or even millions of years ago. Mastodon remains have been found near ancient, dried-up ponds and lakes.

gourds (GORDZ) Gourds are fruits with hard rinds that grow on a vine, such as pumpkins or squash. Mastodons sometimes ate wild gourds.

insulate (IN-suh-layt) To insulate is to cover something with a material that helps keep it warm or cold. Underneath the skin of a woolly mammoth was a thick layer of fat that helped insulate the animal.

mammals (MAM-uhlz) Mammals are animals that are warm-blooded, have backbones, and feed their young with milk made by the bodies of the mothers. Mastodons were elephant-like mammals that lived from about 35 million to 10,000 years ago.

predators (PRED-uh-torz) Predators are animals that hunt and eat other animals. The young mastodons found in a Texas cave were probably killed by predators.

Did You Know?

▸ Scientists have found mastodon bones that were carved by humans thousands of years ago. This means that human beings might have hunted mastodons, eaten them, and made their bones into tools.

▸ Deep inside a cave in France, there are more than 150 paintings of mammoths made by people thousands of years ago. The best and most complete mammoth painting has been nicknamed the Grandfather.

▸ The mammoth is the state fossil of Alaska, Nebraska, and Washington.

▸ Before the mastodon became Michigan's state fossil, a group of middle school students worked hard to bring the beast to everyone's attention. They told lawmakers their reasons for wanting to make it the state fossil. They also raised money for museum programs about the animal.

How to Learn More

AT THE LIBRARY

Giblin, James Cross. *The Mystery of the Mammoth Bones and How It Was Solved.*
New York: HarperCollins Publishers, 1999.

Lambert, David, Darren Naish, and Elizabeth Wyse. *Dinosaur Encyclopedia:*
From Dinosaurs to the Dawn of Man. New York: Dorling Kindersley, 2001.

Palmer, Douglas, Barry Cox (editor). *The Simon & Schuster Encyclopedia of Dinosaurs & Prehistoric*
Creatures: A Visual Who's Who of Prehistoric Life. New York: Simon & Schuster, 1999.

ON THE WEB

Visit our home page for lots of links about mammoths and mastodons:

http://www.childsworld.com/links.html

NOTE TO PARENTS, TEACHERS, AND LIBRARIANS: We routinely verify our Web links
to make sure they're safe, active sites—so encourage your readers to check them out!

PLACES TO VISIT OR CONTACT

AMERICAN MUSEUM OF NATURAL HISTORY
To view one of the most complete mastodon
skeletons ever found, along with many
other fossils of ancient mammals
Central Park West at 79th Street
New York, NY 10024-5192
212/769-5100

CARNEGIE MUSEUM OF NATURAL HISTORY
To see a variety of fossils of extinct animals
4400 Forbes Avenue
Pittsburgh, PA 15213
412/622-3131

MAMMOTH SITE OF HOT SPRINGS, SOUTH DAKOTA
To see many mammoth fossils and
tour an active fossil dig site
1800 West Highway 18 By-Pass
Hot Springs, SD 57747
605/745-6017

MASTODON STATE HISTORIC SITE
To learn more about mastodons and the Native
American groups that may have hunted them
1050 Museum Drive
Imperial, MO 63052
800/334-6946

SMITHSONIAN NATIONAL MUSEUM OF
NATURAL HISTORY
To learn more about mammoths, mastodons,
and other Ice Age mammals
10th Street and Constitution Avenue NW
Washington, DC 20560-0166
202/357-2700

The Geologic Time Scale

CAMBRIAN PERIOD

Date: 540 million to 505 million years ago
Most major animal groups appeared by the end of this period. Trilobites were common and algae became more diversified.

ORDOVICIAN PERIOD

Date: 505 million to 440 million years ago
Marine life became more diversified. Crinoids and blastoids appeared, as did corals and primitive fish. The first land plants appeared. The climate changed greatly during this period—it began as warm and moist, but temperatures ultimately dropped. Huge glaciers formed, causing sea levels to fall.

SILURIAN PERIOD

Date: 440 million to 410 million years ago
Glaciers melted, sea levels rose, and Earth's climate became more stable. Plants with vascular systems developed. This means they had parts that helped them conduct food and water.

DEVONIAN PERIOD

Date: 410 million to 360 million years ago
Fish became more diverse, as did land plants. The first trees and forests appeared at this time, and the earliest seed-bearing plants began to grow. The first land-living vertebrates and insects appeared. Fossils also reveal evidence of the first ammonoids and amphibians. The climate was warm and mild.

CARBONIFEROUS PERIOD

Date: 360 million to 286 million years ago
The climate was warm and humid, but cooled toward the end of the period. Coal swamps dotted the landscape, as did a multitude of ferns. The earliest reptiles appeared on Earth. Pelycosaurs such as *Edaphosaurus* evolved toward the end of the Carboniferous period.

PERMIAN PERIOD

Date: 286 million to 248 million years ago
Algae, sponges, and corals were common on the ocean floor. Amphibians and reptiles were also prevalent at this time, as were seed-bearing plants and conifers. However, this period ended with the largest mass extinction on Earth. This may have been caused by volcanic activity or the formation of glaciers and the lowering of sea levels.

TRIASSIC PERIOD

Date: 248 million to 208 million years ago
The climate during this period was warm and dry. The first true mammals appeared, as did frogs, salamanders, and lizards. Evergreen trees made up much of the plant life. The first dinosaurs, including *Coelophysis*, existed on Earth. In the skies, pterosaurs became the earliest winged reptiles to take flight. In the seas, ichthyosaurs and plesiosaurs made their appearance.

JURASSIC PERIOD

Date: 208 million to 144 million years ago

The climate of the Jurassic period was warm and moist. The first birds appeared at this time, and plant life was more diverse and widespread. Although dinosaurs didn't even exist in the beginning of the Triassic period, they ruled Earth by Jurassic times. *Allosaurus, Apatosaurus, Archaeopteryx, Brachiosaurus, Compsognathus, Diplodocus, Ichthyosaurus, Plesiosaurus,* and *Stegosaurus* were just a few of the prehistoric creatures that lived during this period.

CRETACEOUS PERIOD

Date: 144 million to 65 million years ago

The climate of the Cretaceous period was fairly mild. Many modern plants developed, including those with flowers. With flowering plants came a greater diversity of insect life. Birds further developed into two types: flying and flightless. Prehistoric creatures such as *Ankylosaurus, Edmontosaurus, Iguanodon, Maiasaura, Oviraptor, Psittacosaurus, Spinosaurus, Triceratops, Troodon, Tyrannosaurus rex,* and *Velociraptor* all existed during this period. At the end of the Cretaceous period came a great mass extinction that wiped out the dinosaurs, along with many other groups of animals.

TERTIARY PERIOD

Date: 65 million to 1.8 million years ago

Mammals were extremely diversified at this time, and modern-day creatures such as horses, dogs, cats, bears, and whales developed.

QUATERNARY PERIOD

Date: 1.8 million years ago to today

Temperatures continued to drop during this period. Several periods of glacial development led to what is known today as the Ice Age. Prehistoric creatures such as glyptodonts, mammoths, mastodons, *Megatherium,* and saber-toothed cats roamed Earth. A mass extinction of these animals occurred approximately 10,000 years ago. The first human beings evolved during the Quaternary period.

Index

About the Author

Susan H. Gray has bachelor's and master's degrees in zoology
and has taught college-level courses in biology. She first fell in love
with fossil hunting while studying paleontology in college. In her
25 years as an author, she has written many articles for scientists
and researchers, and many science books for children. Susan enjoys
gardening, traveling, and playing the piano. She and her husband,
Michael, live in Cabot, Arkansas.